The Rain Fo

by Michèle Dufresne

Pioneer Valley Educational Press, Inc.

Look at the rain forest.

The tropical rain forest is a forest of trees in a tropical region around the equator. The climate is almost always hot and wet.

3

Look at the vines.
The vines are in the rain forest.

As it grows, a vine sends down roots to the forest floor. The roots spread and put out branches that twine around the host tree. After many years, the host tree dies. The dead tree rots away and leaves a hollow network of stems.

Look at the bird.
The bird is in the rain forest.

Here is a blue and gold Macaw. Macaws are colorful parrots that live in the rain forest. They are an endangered bird due to the shrinking of rain forests and the illegal trapping of the birds.

Look at the ferns.
The ferns are in the rain forest.

Look at the frog.
The frog is in the rain forest.

This is a Red-Eyed Tree Frog. The frog's bright coloring is a defense mechanism against predators. When a predator swoops down, the frog opens its bright, red eyes and frightens the predator.

Look at the monkey.
The monkey is in the rain forest.

This small White-Faced Monkey eats fruit and insects. They are not afraid of humans and won't hesitate to hiss or even throw things at people.

Look at the rain forest.
What can you see?

The Rain Forest

bird

fern

frog

monkey

vine